T0129055

Everywhere an Angel

A Journey of Love, Faith, Laughter, and Heartbreak

Thom Barrett

Order this book online at www.trafford.com
or email orders@trafford.com

Most Trafford titles are also available at major online book retailers.

Printed in the United States of America.

ISBN: 978-1-4907-3543-6 (sc)
ISBN: 978-1-4907-3542-9 (hc)
ISBN: 978-1-4907-3544-3 (e)

Library of Congress Control Number: 2014908319

Trafford rev. 05/02/2014

 www.trafford.com

North America & international
toll-free: 1 888 232 4444 (USA & Canada)
fax: 812 355 4082

In memory of my wonderful and loving wife of forty-seven years, who dedicated every day trying to make our lives as normal as could be under the circumstances.

Also, to all the people who helped us along our journey. Without their help, support, and prayers, we would not have survived.

A special thanks to Morris and Jerri Blumenthal who were always there when we needed them and stuck with us through the good, the bad, and the ugly for the past thirty years.

Morris and Jerri Blumenthal

Preface

While raising our boys, Ty (Thom) and Andy, many people suggested that I write a book, but I never seriously considered it.

Recently, on a one-month road trip distributing the cremains of my wife, Lynda, and visiting family and friends, writing a book came up twice.

While visiting my nephew Michael Messemer in East Hampton, New York, on Long Island, he told me that he had collaborated on a book and that I should consider writing one as well because of our boys.

I was also told by his mother, my sister Maryalice, that I should consider writing a book about my life with Lynda and the many complications that occurred in our lives.

Maryalice had just bought a brand-new baby grand piano and did not know how to play. I told her I would make a deal with her. When I returned home, I would start the book if she would learn to play the piano. She agreed.

I was home about three days and woke one night about 3:00 a.m. feeling very lonely and sad in my empty home, so I decided to write.

The next day, I called Maryalice to tell her I had begun the book, and I wanted to know if she had started practicing the piano. Her answer was "no."

I wish I could tell you that Maryalice will be appearing at a concert hall near you soon, but she isn't quite there yet.

It would be nice if I could tell you that I had some very altruistic motives for writing this book, but I didn't.

However, I did find it very comforting to write and, in doing so, filled a tremendous void in my life since Lynda died. It gave me a good reason to get up each morning.

Having completed it, I hope that our life story might help some family going through similar trials.

The only advice I feel comfortable giving to everyone is to accept God's gifts. They are out there. You just have to pay attention to what is going on around you.

I give this advice not because I always paid attention, but while writing this book, I realized what God has given us and that he has always been there, whether we thought so at the time or not.

Whether they manifest themselves as real angels or human beings acting like angels, I believe angels are more involved in our lives than we give them credit.

In this book, you will witness angels appearing in all forms: people doing angels' work, phenomena only unseen angels could accomplish, and an actual encounter with an angel.

I believe almost everyone mentioned in my book qualifies under one of the above categories—some are just more obvious than others.

It would be impossible to calculate the number of times in our lives that angels interceded, and it never occurred to us that it was not just a matter of luck, but an outside influence.

Prologue

efore I escort you through our journey, I would like to give you some insight into the character of our ship's captain—my wife of forty-seven years and my constant angel, Lynda Schmitt Barrett. I also need to give you some background on myself.

She always had a strong sense of family and friends that started as a young girl. Lynda spent all her summers growing up at a beach house in Hampton Bays in Long Island, New York, and, as a result, had a great love of anything connected with the sea.

At ten years old, she could bring their boat through the locks at Shinnecock Canal by herself so that she could fish with her father and grandfather in Peconic Bay. She also loved to go clamming off the beach in front of their house.

While working on "Everywhere An Angel" it struck me how much our lives are based on small building blocks that might seem inconsequential at the time.

In 1945 Lynda's Father nicknamed her 'Winnie' based on Winnie the Pooh. In 1968 I named our sail boat "Winnie." All this so I could use "Out of my sight" in Lynda's eulogy and pull it all together with Bon Voyage "Winnie" in 2013.

February 5th 2014 was our 48th wedding anniversary and it has given me another opportunity to reflect on our life together.

Lynda was the most unselfish person you would ever meet. She always placed her needs after those of family and friends. If someone needed something and it meant she had to give something up for them to get it she did it with a smile. I know that this gave her more pleasure than if she had gotten what she wanted. I learned a great deal from Lynda about giving.

Waterskiing and sailing were among her favorite things to do. She was accomplished at both of these, and I am told she even skied on her neighbor's shoulders once.

Lynda was extremely competitive in sports and loved field hockey in college and tennis as she got older. She was told at her first tennis lesson that the backhand was the easiest shot in tennis, so she had no trepidation using it as opposed to most people who will run around to avoid hitting their backhand. Pity the person at the net when Lynda returned a shot using her backhand.

The competitive spirit proved to be most beneficial when she would advocate for the boys. She was aggressive in pursuing every benefit available to them, and I liked to call her "the velvet hammer." She got it all done with a smile, which was disarming.

She was a successful businesswoman and was always fair in all her endeavors.

Religion was very important to her and when she signed the agreement to raise our children in the Catholic faith it became a lifelong plan for her to see that the boys get the best Catholic training she could find for them. I cannot count the number of times she was the leader in the family when it came to getting the boys involved in their faith and if it had been up to me I probably would have let it slide.

Her friendships were very important to her and everyone who got to know her loved her.

I have tried to come up with some special things that she did for us and am having difficulty isolating things she did and I believe that it is because they were always done so casually and without fanfare and she made them seem so natural and effortless that you wouldn't notice that it required a sacrifice on her part.

When I told the priest that Lynda and I both wanted to be remarried in the Catholic Church as soon as possible after the Episcopal service, this was not me speaking for Lynda, this was really the way she felt and I believe that if her mother had not been so adamantly against the Catholic faith that Lynda would have converted to Catholicism immediately. Lynda did convert soon after her mother passed away.

Although Lynda sensed that my mother was not her biggest fan for the first five years of our marriage, there was never a question as to whether my mother would be included in our lives whenever possible. Lynda decided from day one that she was not going to let mother deter her from seeing to it that our boys know both their grandmothers. Lynda was always the one to remind me that it had been a while since I called my mother and would mention it until I did so.

During all the years our mothers were alive, her mother lived to be 83 and my mother died at 99, the only times I remember them together was at each of our fathers funerals, and that didn't go well.

I can't remember whether it was my father's funeral or her father's but Lynda and I both spoke to our respective mothers and told them that they must call each other by their first names when greeting each other. They both agreed so when they met at the funeral parlor my mother said, "hello Mildred" and Lynda's mother said, "hello Mrs. Barrett." Lynda again stressed that she was to call my mother Helen so when they said goodbye Lynda's mother said "goodbye Helen" and my mother said, "goodbye Mrs. Schmitt." Another attempt to get them together in the same room was never made. The only time I can remember them being together was when the boys were sick and they knew that we had enough trouble in our lives at the time so they behaved.

During her last week before she died, she told me who among our single friends would make a good companion for me after she was gone.

Lynda was always the first one to point out to me the most attractive women in the room wherever we went. She believed that just because I was on a diet didn't mean I couldn't look at the menu.

Chapter One

 # Hours to Live

I t was the one call no parent ever wants to receive. Mease Dunedin Hospital in Dunedin, Florida, was calling at 2:00 a.m. to advise us that we should come back to the hospital as soon as possible because our oldest son, Ty, aged thirty-eight, would probably not live through the night.

Ty was mentally and physically challenged and had been living in a medical group home in Pinellas County, Florida, for about seventeen years.

While dressing Ty Friday morning, his caregivers dropped him and, unbeknownst to them at the time, broke the same leg for the third time in thirteen years.

It was not determined that the leg was broken until he returned home from the day-care program he attended every weekday. They had just put him in his wheelchair and sent him off.

This break proved to be too much for Ty. Forty-eight hours after they dropped him, he died.

After the second time Ty broke his leg, we believed he had multiple strokes that left him incontinent, permanently wheelchair-bound, and with very little speech.

During the recovery process, Ty was not getting his appetite back and we were worried that there might be some kind of a stomach problem so we made an appointment with his gastroenterologist, Dr. Howard Klein. Ty had to be transported in a handicapped van because he was in a wheelchair. When the van arrived at the doctor's office they were unable to get the back of the van opened so Ty was unable to go into the office.

When I went into the office and explained the problem to the staff they consulted with Dr. Klein and the next thing I knew he was on his way to the van to examine Ty in the parking lot. I believe most doctors would have had us reschedule another appointment. Another angel, only this one came with a stethoscope.

Ty's neurologist said that if you only viewed Ty's brain scans, you would believe that he was in a vegetative state because of all the damage he had sustained over his lifetime.

Not only was Ty not in a vegetative state, but he had a sense of humor, smiled, and was happy most of the time.

The broken legs only complicated a very complicated condition that I will discuss later.

Let me back up. Ty's legal name on his birth certificate is Thomas Aloysius Barrett III. This means that he was initially also called Thom.

Lynda's mother, Mildred Schmitt, was dating and eventually engaged. Her fiancee felt in order to eliminate the confusion of little Thom and big Thom, he nicknamed our son Ty, and it obviously stuck.

I mention this because my parents' first child was a boy whom they named Thomas Barrett Jr. My brother was dropped by a caregiver when he was an infant and died. I assume my parents were set on having an heir named Thomas, so they also named me Thomas Aloysius Barrett Jr., although not really the correct thing to do.

Life plays strange tricks on us when you consider that my brother, Thomas, was dropped by a caregiver as an infant, which caused his death; and my son Thomas suffered the same fate—only at the age of thirty-eight, eighty years later.

While writing about my brother, Thom, I believe I might have had a small epiphany.

My sisters have always said that I was my parents' favorite and that their brother was an "only child."

Maybe the fact that our parents gave me the same name as their deceased firstborn caused them to be overly protective of me.

If, in fact, I was the favorite child, it was not because of something my sisters did or didn't do, but because I was named after a lost child. We never forget our children who die before us.

I hope people will understand our feelings at the moment we received the call about Ty. We wanted Ty to go to God and be freed of all the mental and physical shackles that had restricted him almost his entire life. He lived thirty-eight years—thirty-five and one-half which were hell.

As a priest friend of ours said when Ty died, he was a saint and rode the express train to the right hand of God because of the way he conducted his life and how much he taught so many people.

Ty contracted Reye's syndrome when he was two and a half years old, which left him with a paralysis on the left side of his body, speech-impaired, mentally impaired, and with a seizure disorder.

Chapter Two

Friendships

Lynda passed away in June of 2013. She died of complications of multiple fatal diseases. She is a saint and never presented as ill as she was. She had great faith in God and believed that He was always with us, no matter how bad things appeared.

When we married in 1966, we lived in Tudor City in New York City, which is at Forty-Third Street and First Avenue, across from the United Nations building. A month later, we moved to Asheville, North Carolina, which began a series of moves over our lifetime together involving my career.

Despite our moves to various states, Lynda made sure that I always scheduled time with three great guys whom I met in 1948 when my family moved to the Bronx. I was eleven. It was right after a heavy snowstorm, and my three new friends thought a good way to welcome the new kid to the neighborhood would be a three-on-one snowball fight. Obviously, I was getting the worst of the deal, so Matt Cavanagh came over to my side to make things even. Matt, Bill Mulderig, Charlie Garvin, and I became fast friends for life. Bill Mulderig and I were extremely competitive with each other, whether it be an organized sport or just some sort of pickup game.

Bill was better at baseball and basketball, and I was better at football, golf, and tennis—but Bill always won the big competition. The girls were crazy about him all through his life. He was "Peck's Bad Boy," and the girls loved him for that.

When we lived in Atlanta, Bill called and said he would be in town with his business partner and could I play tennis with them, did I have a club we could play at, and would I get a partner to play doubles with for the next week. I said yes to all three.

Remember how I said Bill and I competed at everything and were always trying to go one up on the other? Well, this was an opportunity I could not resist. Not only did I get someone to be my partner, but he was the club tennis pro, and his name was Carlton Davis. Needless to say, we beat them handily: 6-0, 6-1. When we got to the net to shake hands, Bill said that he really needed to take some lessons. I suggested Bill talk to Carlton about lessons because he was the club pro. Bill looked at me, shook his head, and said "Well played!" and proceeded to get hysterical. (Those were not quite his exact words, but in an attempt to maintain the spirit of the book, I thought it would be appropriate to clean up his response. But he really did laugh.) He was able to finally say he wished he had thought of getting a pro. One up for Thom!

Whenever we saw each other after that, the tennis match in Atlanta always came up, and we would both laugh. Bill died of cancer in 2010 and is sorely missed by all who knew and loved him.

Carlton became more than the tennis pro at the club to our family. He became a great friend to all of us.

Although nothing would ever come of it, he gave both of our boys free tennis lessons which helped them feel that they were just like their peers who participated in sports. One of Lynda's many goals for the boys was to let them experience what their friends did and Carlton contributed to this a great deal.

Andy actually became very proficient at the game considering his handicap. He wasn't going to win any tournaments but he could return the ball on a regular basis, which is a lot more than I can say for some people without a handicap.

When we moved to Clearwater, we used to spend a lot of time with the boys on the tennis court and one day Andy's pediatrician saw Andy playing tennis and asked us why we made him play because he had a visual impairment and had trouble seeing the ball when he hit from his backhand side. We explained that this was Andy's choice and once Bob saw how much Andy loved the game and how good he was he completely understood.

Andy also became pretty good at golf and many a Saturday morning, he and or Ty would ride with me when I played with my friends. I do not think that there a lot of men who would be comfortable with the boys around during their Saturday golf game but it got to the point that if one of them were not there on Saturday the guys were concerned. More angels . . .

A great example of parents exposing their child with special needs to everything in life, happened one day at a public tennis facility in a park in Atlanta. Lynda and I watched a pre teen boy with severe Cerebral Palsy practice his tennis and after every shot he hit he would lose his balance and fall to the ground. He wore knee pads to protect himself. This obviously didn't bother him because he got up each time with a smile on his face and resumed practice. What a special young man and how special his parents must be to encourage him.

Almost every Saturday when we lived in Atlanta I played tennis in a city wide league called *The Atlanta Lawn Tennis Association*. Lynda, Ty and Andy came to almost all of the matches played, as did members of the other players' families and after each competition we would all go to a fun restaurant for lunch. The guys all adopted the boys and treated them as they did any other kids in the group. Andy became particularly friendly with two of the guys Paul McNaughton and Tom Beddoe. Andy has remained great friends with Paul. Paul at his expense has often flown Andy to Atlanta and entertained him for a week or so. More angels . . . When I go to Atlanta I see Paul and Tom and we play golf. Tennis is a little more strenuous than what we are up to.

Lynda never let me forget how precious and rare longtime friendships are and that it sometimes required an extra effort to maintain them. I am so glad she did. Matt, Charlie, and I are still the best of friends, and it has been sixty-five years since we first met on Marion Avenue in the Bronx.

Chapter Three

House on Marion Avenue

The house we moved to in the Bronx in 1947 had been in the family for about sixty years, and my mother had been raised there. My father had lived less than a block away.

Our new home was the last of three private homes on the block. The rest had been torn down and apartment buildings had been built.

In 1953, Matt Cavanagh, one of my snowball friends, was at home lamenting that there was nothing to do. Just then, he heard the fire engines and ran out of his home to see where the fire was. Much to his surprise, it was my house, and there was no one at home but my younger sister, Sheila. She was sitting at the curb clutching our dog in one arm and the parakeet cage in the other. Matt asked Sheila where our parents were, and she said they were at a cocktail party and gave him the phone number.

Matt called and asked to speak to my mother. When she got on the phone, Matt informed her that the house was on fire. She asked if the fire department was there and did it seem to be under control. He said yes to both. She thanked him for calling and went back to the party. Obviously, Mother loved a good party. Later, my father asked her what the call was, and she told him the house was on fire and that it seemed to be under control. My father decided it was important enough to go home and see what was going on.

This was a three-story house, and when my father got there, the roof had burned off, and there was a tremendous amount of water and smoke damage on all three floors. He then called my mother and told her what was going on at the house. She decided maybe it was time to come home, mostly because she was having dinner guests that night.

My father was a car salesman all his life and had just sold a new car to the couple coming for dinner. He called them to tell them about the fire, but all the dinner guest could talk about was the crack in the windshield of his new car and what could be done about it. After my father explained about the fire for the third time, he finally heard him.

As I said, my mother loved a party and had her guests to dinner seven hours after the fire. They had deli takeout by candlelight.

Although my mother's lack of an appropriate response in almost losing our home and the welfare of her children, I believe that she taught me a lesson about how to stay calm under all circumstances and how to handle adversities in life.

Later on in life when I was going through many crises with the boys I was able to draw on her response and appropriately handle them with calmness.

Another life lesson I learned while living on Marion Ave. was taught to me by a boy a few years younger than me, who lived across the street. I believe he was autistic but at that age I was not aware of what that meant.

All I knew was that he was a nice kid who could not talk and loved to play catch in the street. He had a great arm and could throw a ball a lot farther and accurately than older kids. At least a couple of days a week he would knock on our door and without speaking, indicate that he wanted to play ball. Looking back I realize that this relationship helped me with my own two handicapped boys and helped prepare me in handling their frustrations. Oddly enough this boy's name was also Tom but we called him Tommy.

When the house was being rebuilt, we three children were farmed out to the various relatives for three months.

The house was eventually sold in 1955 so they could build another apartment building, but they retained our street number.

The house that my father lived in around the corner from my mother when they were growing up was called the castle by the people in the neighborhood. It was a huge three-story, six-bedroom house, which was needed to accommodate my grandparents and their eight children. They also owned a spacious summer home in Connecticut.

My grandfather had an exclusive contract with General Motors to sell Buicks in the borough of the Bronx and had three dealerships. This was prior to WWII, so needless to say, they were quite comfortable.

My father graduated from Fordham Prep and had a football scholarship to Notre Dame but chose not to accept it. First of all, he thought his future was secure in the family business, and secondly, he was in love with a Ziegfeld girl and didn't want to leave her. The family was lucky enough to survive the Stock Market Crash of 1929 but could not survive the effects of WWII on the automobile business.

The family put everything they had back into the business during the war because they knew that after the war, they would again be back on top.

The problem with this was that my grandfather passed away six months before the war ended, and General Motors would not renew the contract with my father and his brother because, by this time, all their assets had been depleted while attempting to stay open during the war.

The great thing about moving back to my parents' neighborhood was my new friends knew all about my family and their previous lifestyle. The Barretts used to give every child at St. Philip Neri grammar school a gift at Christmas. My friends all remembered this.

I loved my father a great deal. He was a very kind and gentle man, and he taught me a great deal about life. The problem was that he was constantly chasing the pot of gold at the end of the rainbow, hoping to achieve great wealth again. It never happened. My father had a heart attack in his car in a parking lot and never regained consciousness at the hospital.

My wife, Lynda, told me that she saw tears run down his cheeks when I entered his hospital room. As we have said many times in our lives, you never know how much people in a coma are aware of in terms of what is going on around them.

Chapter Four

Santa Claus

I n 1960 I finished college and decided to sell life insurance. I tried it for four months and hated going to work every day. I am a good salesman but not good at cold-calling and couldn't handle the phone work.

Rather than wait to be drafted, I decided to enlist in the National Guard and go on active duty for six months as required.

When I enlisted in October, I was told there would not be anyone assigned to active duty until after the holidays. I was now going to be unemployed for at least three months and needed a temporary job.

When I was in college, I went in to New York City to try to get work for the holidays and had been offered a job as Santa Claus. I was mortified! I have always been self-conscious about my weight and felt I had been offered a position because of my size. A week or so later, I decided that I would have been a great Santa and regretted my decision.

One day after resigning from life insurance sales, I was looking through the help-wanted ads, and there was a position available as Santa Claus at Macy's Department Store in White Plains, New York, about twenty minutes from my home. I never forgot how badly I felt after refusing the job in New York City four years earlier, so I submitted an application.

When I interviewed with the personnel director, she expressed surprise that a man of twenty-three would be interested in the position. I explained that I was going in the service in January and needed a temporary job through the holidays. I explained that I had once been offered a job as Santa and always regretted not accepting it. I told her I loved kids and was really good with them.

She informed me that they had interviewed a senior citizen who would be more age-appropriate, but he had to pass a physical to get the job. The reason for the physical was that lifting all the children onto his lap could be strenuous, and they had to be sure his heart could handle the stress.

I was surprised when the personnel director called to inform me that the senior citizen failed the physical. She asked if I was still interested. If so, the position was mine.

As Santa, lunch break was two hours, so I was able to go to my sister Maryalice's for lunch since she lived only ten minutes from the store. One day while I was there, Maryalice told me that her three-year-old daughter Sue had accidentally broken a lamp in the morning.

Later that day, Maryalice brought her four kids to see Santa, and when Sue got on Santa's lap, I asked her if she had been a good girl. She said yes, she had. I then said to her that I was sure she had been, and I knew she didn't mean to break the lamp that morning. You should have seen the look on her face!

Maryalice said from that day on until Christmas, whenever the kids started to act up and get out of hand, all she had to do was remind them Santa had known Sue broke the lamp and he was watching them all.

I saw eleven thousand children in five weeks, so I understand why it was important that a physical be taken by senior applicants.

I not only had children sit on my lap, but also grandmas because they wanted to send a picture of themselves sitting on the lap of their good friend, Santa, to their grandchildren and tell them that they had put in a good word for them.

One of my favorite stories about being Santa was the time triplets came to have their picture taken with Santa. If there were just two children, I could pin each of their arms to my side and hold the other arm with my free hand so they couldn't get frisky. Three children were a problem. The third boy stood between my legs, and both his hands were free. He thought it would be a good idea to run across the room with my beard in hand. It was on a piece of elastic, so when he pulled it off, he got it about two inches from my face and it snapped back over my eyes. Needless to say, from then on, I glued it to my face!

While driving home late one night, I got pulled over by a state trooper for a broken taillight. When I gave the officer my license, he proceeded to print my name on the ticket. While completing the ticket, he asked me what I did for a living, and I told him I was Santa Claus at Macy's. He looked at me dismayed and said, "How can I go home and face my kids after giving Santa a ticket?" But once the ticket was started, it could not be stopped or altered. He then told me that he would set a court date for January 10. I told him that I would be unable to make that date because I was going in the army on January 6. This was probably the only time in his career that he truly regretted issuing a ticket.

Chapter Five

Fort Dix, New Jersey

As anyone who has been through basic training will tell you, no one goes on sick call just before you qualify on the firing range. If you miss qualifying, you are recycled to a unit just starting basic training and you have to repeat the first weeks of basic. I was no different. I had pneumonia, and delaying sick call only made it worse.

I finally qualified and went to the hospital and was there for almost two weeks. This was February and it was freezing cold, and we had a lot of snow that year at Fort Dix.

When I returned to the barracks the afternoon I was discharged from the hospital, I reported to my sergeant for two weeks' light duty as prescribed by the hospital. He assigned me to fire watch that night. Fire watch consisted of making sure the coal furnaces in the eight barracks of the company were burning all the time and putting new coals on them on a regular basis as needed.

The sergeant said before I started fire watch that I was to call my family and let them know I was out of the hospital. My mother answered the phone, and I told her I was feeling better and was back in my barracks on light duty. She asked me what light duty was comprised of, and I told her I would not be doing regular training with the rest of my platoon. I really didn't want to tell her what I was doing that night, but she persisted, so I did. When we hung up, everything seemed to be all right with her, and I went on fire watch.

Because I had been up all night, I was given the next day off and told to go back to the barracks and get some sleep. The other members of my platoon were in the field, so the barracks were empty. About two hours into my sleep, my sergeant came barreling into the barracks and told me to report to the commanding officer right away.

I proceeded to dress and went to get my winter gear on, and he said to leave them and follow him. I knew I was in trouble but had no idea how bad it was. You were never to leave your barracks unless appropriately attired.

When I walked into the office of my commanding officer, he asked me what I did the previous night and when I told him I called my family, he wanted to know what was said word for word. I told him everything that had been said to my mother and that it ended very calmly. Apparently, it was a facade. My mother, after hanging up, sent a telegram to President Kennedy informing him that her son was receiving "cruel and inhuman treatment" at Fort Dix and that something should be done. President Kennedy forwarded this to the commanding general of Fort Dix with a copy to the inspector general, who in turn called my commanding officer looking for an explanation.

I was never so embarrassed in my life. I was an outcast in my platoon. I felt sorry for the guy who slept above me because his name was Barrett as well, and he got some of the grief intended for me.

After two weeks of light duty, I was on KP after the fire watch incident. I had to go back to the hospital for x-rays to determine if the pneumonia was gone. The x-rays showed that I still had pneumonia, and I was given the option of going back to the hospital or returning to my barracks for two more weeks of light duty. I chose to return to my barracks with another two weeks of light duty. Not only was I on light duty, I was on no duty. I stayed in my barracks for two weeks and only went outside to go to meals. It finally cleared up after the second two weeks of light duty.

After boot camp, I was supposed to be stationed at Fort Leonard Wood, Missouri, but my orders were changed, and I stayed at Fort Dix for the remainder of my six months. I was an "on-the-job" trainee in the quartermaster's corps distributing uniforms to incoming recruits, but there were never any incoming recruits. I had my own barracks for the rest of my tour. Eighty bunks, twenty toilets, ten sinks, and twelve showers—all to myself!

I once asked a sergeant when I was getting out, why no one bothered with me after my second pneumonia, and he told me that after I got sick again, they stamped PI in bold letters all over my personnel file. PI means "political influence" and to "leave him alone."

At the time, Fort Dix was in the news a lot, and they didn't need more headlines about recruits dying. A day after the telegram was sent, I was having chow in the mess hall when the guy next to me asked me if I had heard about the guy who sent a telegram to President Kennedy. I said, "Wasn't that really dumb? I couldn't believe anyone would be that stupid."

Chapter Six

Tucson

W hen I was discharged from active duty in July of 1962, I moved to Tucson, Arizona, because a college classmate of mine had moved there for health reasons and said it was a great place to live. I was single, had no career direction, and had always wanted to travel to the West, so I went.

I mentioned this to some buddies while in the army, and they asked if they could hitch a ride, and once we got to Tucson, they would go their separate ways. This was fine with me because I wasn't looking forward to the long drive by myself. Besides, I had very little money and could use the help with expenses.

My uncle owned a 1951 Ford and offered to sell it to me for one dollar if this would help get me started. This was the little extra push I needed.

We took about four days to complete the trip and mostly slept in the car at night.

After two days, we stopped at a service station outside of LaGrange, Indiana, to fuel up, and the wires under the dashboard shorted and caught fire.

After pushing the car away from the pumps, we were able to extinguish the fire before it did too much damage.

We had the car towed to a service station in town, and they gave us an estimate to repair the wiring of five hundred dollars. I believe all they could see was three guys in a car with New York plates and thought the gravy train had just arrived. Considering we didn't have two hundred dollars between us, this was not an option.

The three of us decided that we would go to the post office and ship our belongings to our destinations and hitchhike the rest of the way. When we told the mechanic our plan, he said that he would revisit the estimate and get back to us. His new estimate was fifty dollars, and off we went to Tucson with our repaired vehicle.

When I lived in Tucson, I worked for a finance company trying to get a very peace-loving tribe to pay their bills. No matter what threats I made, it didn't faze them. It was like water off a duck's back.

The interest rate they were paying was exorbitant. I started to side with the Indians and became ineffective at my job, and after one and one-half years, I returned to New York. By the way, I had to fly back because my car died in Tucson.

As with most single men, my roommate and I were always interested in meeting girls. One night, a girl called to speak to me and said that we had a mutual friend who suggested she call me, and did I have a friend so that we could double date. I said yes, and we all went out the next night and had a great time. I kept pressing her for the name of the mutual friend, but she wouldn't tell me.

After a few dates, she confessed that since she and her friend both worked for the local paper, they placed an ad in the help-wanted section and had resumes sent to their own PO box. They then culled out the ones that showed promise and threw out the rest. They then called the interesting ones using the "mutual friend" routine. I thought that this was really ingenious.

Almost six years after I left Tucson, I accidentally ran into my old roommate at a turnstile in Grand Central Station. We had never communicated this whole time but were delighted to see each other. I invited him to a going-away party at my sister's because I was moving in a week. Sorry to say he got sick and was not able to come. We never saw each other again.

Chapter Seven

Advertising Career

The reason I went into advertising was upon the recommendation of a good friend, Tom Leahy. Tom was also a friend from the Bronx, and he was selling TV time for CBS TV in New York City. I was floundering and didn't know what I wanted to do at the time when I returned from Tucson.

Tom went on to achieve great success at CBS, and one of the positions he was promoted to was vice president of daytime sales.

When he was promoted, I had my secretary send him the following telegram comprised of all the CBS soaps on the air in the early seventies:

Congratulations to the King of the Soaps. I hope "As the World Turns" in your "Search for Tomorrow" your "Love of Life" will be your "Guiding Light" even beyond "The Edge of Night" regardless of your own "Secret Storm" and that you will always remember that "Love is a Many Splendid Thing."

I visited Tom at his home twenty years later, and the telegram was framed over his desk. In December of 1998, he sent me a copy before he died.

Chapter Eight

The Meeting

I was a buyer of TV and radio time at a large advertising agency in New York City when Lynda and I met.

Dick Ullman—a salesman who called on me and worked with Lynda—told me there was a very attractive single girl in his office and that I should meet her.

I was twenty-eight years old and single. I had met some great people this way, so I said yes.

The next time Dick called me, he had the call transferred to Lynda. We had a great conversation and made a date for that evening after work.

Later, I received an invitation from another salesman to go out on his clients' fifty-foot yacht docked on the Hudson River, so I called Lynda and broke the date. Lynda knew the business we were in and was very understanding. We made a date for the next night, and as they say, "That's all she wrote!" I never dated another woman. Thank God Lynda gave me a second chance.

Of course, for the rest of our lives, Lynda loved to tell the story that I canceled our first date because I got a better offer. She called me the "King of the Better Offer."

We met at Sardis East the next night, which was August 15, 1965. We got engaged at Thanksgiving and married on February 5, 1966, but not without complications.

After we moved to Asheville, we never saw Dick until ten years later. We were at dinner at Brennan's in Atlanta celebrating our tenth anniversary, and Dick was sitting across the room. He had changed careers, moved to Atlanta, and had a distributorship at the Merchandise Mart. He asked Lynda if she would like to come work for him. We had just sent Ty to Stewart and could use the additional income. A coincidence? I don't think so.

Chapter Nine

The Weddings

Iam Catholic and Lynda was Episcopalian at the time. Her parents were not affiliated with any church, but her mother had a strong dislike for the Catholic Church. I never found out why.

When I met with her mother and father to ask for her hand in marriage, we told them we wanted to marry in the Catholic Church. Lynda's mother very calmly informed us that if we did get married in the Catholic Church, Lynda would no longer be involved in their lives. I believe she meant this and had to assume the worst. I loved Lynda and she loved me. Our goal was to be married and keep our families intact. After discussing the ramifications with Lynda, we decided to be married in the Episcopalian Church and, as soon as possible, remarried in the Catholic Church. I felt God would forgive me, but I didn't think Lynda's mother would forgive her.

This created a problem with my side of the family. The church did not approve of a Catholic being married outside the church and forbade Catholics to attend the ceremony.

This meant that my parents, relatives, and friends could not attend the Episcopal service. This did not mean my parents did not acknowledge the marriage. As a matter of fact, my mother, father, aunt, and uncle met us at the airport for a celebratory drink just before we boarded our flight to Puerto Rico for our honeymoon.

My mother and her sister married brothers, so my aunt was also Mrs. Barrett. When my mother introduced my wife to my aunt, she said, "Mrs. Barrett, I would like you to meet Mrs. Barrett."

Once we decided to have the formal wedding at the Episcopal Church, I went on a mission to find someone who would remarry us in the Catholic Church, even if it could be done later that day, before or after the reception. This was not as easy as I thought.

I spent weeks trying to accomplish this goal but to no avail. A week before the wedding, I was discussing my problem with another salesman who called on me, and he said he might be able to help. He had a friend who was a Franciscan who taught in New York City every Tuesday night. He arranged for me to meet his friend the next night after his class.

I explained to Father John what my problem was and what I was trying to accomplish. Time was running out because we were to be married on Saturday. Father John told me he was unable to personally help me, but he had a friend who was a priest at Saint Ignatius at Fourteenth Street and Fifth Avenue, and did I have time to visit with him that night even though it was after 10:00 p.m.

We knocked on the rectory door, and Father John asked if we could see Joe Hawes. We were escorted to Father Hawes's office, and when he came in, Father John said I was a friend of his and had a problem he felt Father Hawes could help me resolve. At that point, Father John shook hands with us both and left. I never saw him again but am eternally grateful for what he did for a total stranger.

I then explained to Father Hawes that I was getting married in the Episcopal Church on Saturday, and both my wife and I wanted to be remarried in the Catholic Church as soon as possible, even on the same day. Father Joe said expediency was not necessary, but more importantly, he wanted me to know that after the Episcopal service I was really married. He did not want this issue to diminish our honeymoon.

Father Joe looked at his calendar and said that since we were honeymooning for a week and could probably use two weeks to adjust to our new routine, that he would remarry us in three weeks, and it would be on the altar.

Father Joe told me that I was six weeks, six months, or six years ahead of the time when an interfaith marriage would be simpler.

Lynda and I went back to see Father Joe on our fifth anniversary to let him know how happy we were and thank him again. When we asked for him at the rectory, we were informed that he had left the priesthood and married. I can only hope that his life was as wonderful as he made ours.

When Lynda died on June 23, 2013, Charlie Garvin went to Mass at St. Ignatius in celebration of her life. He had been best man at the Catholic ceremony.

Chapter Ten

Asheville

We moved to Asheville, North Carolina, because I was offered a position at WLOS-TV as national sales manager. This position required traveling to major markets where large advertising agencies were located, whose clients were interested in placing ads on television to sell their products in the Greenville, Asheville, and Spartanburg TV market. These sales calls were made with a sales representative who called on the buyers on a regular basis and lived in the market where the agencies were located.

It was very unusual for a buyer to go directly to a national sales manager's position, but the station wanted someone who knew the buying process and appeared to have some sales ability. This was a very unique market and required buyers to do more than just look at the number of people watching a particular show but also look at what county they were located in.

Much of the interaction between buyers and station personnel involved dinners and lunches because despite what they said, personal relationships did influence buyers.

Little did I know that when I had lunch with the GSM of WLOS, he was actually interviewing me for the NSM position.

The day after we had lunch, I received a call from the GSM asking me if Lynda and I could fly to Asheville to see the market and meet with the general manager. We flew there right after our honeymoon, and I was hired.

We found an apartment near the station the next day and made arrangements to move to our new home.

We shipped our furniture, and the station personnel were gracious enough to be at the apartment to accept delivery.

Not only did they accept delivery, but they set up the bed, found linens and made the bed, and had a bottle of champagne chilling in the fridge for when we arrived.

We arrived late at night and were tired from the long drive, but when we saw what they had done, we were motivated to make our new home less like a motel, so we started to unpack some more boxes.

About an hour into the unpacking, we found the box containing the bedside lamps, so I crawled under the bed to plug them in. Much to my dismay, there was a tape recorder plugged in under the bed set to use.

When I told Lynda what I found, she told me to stop unpacking and that we were returning to New York the next day. There was no way that she could look these people in the eye if they intended to tape-record a newlywed couple on their first night in their new home.

I suggested we wait to make that decision until the next morning when we could confront them about what they did. Lynda halfheartedly agreed, and we went to bed.

About 3:00 a.m., we were awakened by the sound of Flatt and Scruggs blaring out from under the bed. This was their way of welcoming us to the South. Obviously, the tape recorder was set to play and not record, and we were glad we did not start to repack.

When we told our families we were moving to Asheville, we told each of them that it would be good for us to get some separation from our in-laws, and neither suspected it was them we were talking about.

Actually, it was the best thing that happened to us as a couple. It gave us a great foundation for forty-seven years of wedded bliss and enabled us to really become best friends. We were now in a strange city with no friends, and most of the population was retired.

We made a pact that if ever we decided to divorce, each of us would have to move in with our in-laws. Later on, we added a caveat that the one initiating the divorce would have to take the children. Of course, this was in jest because who would want to move in with their in-laws with two handicapped children? Besides, why would they take us?

Chapter Eleven

My Katz Career

We returned to New York after one and one half years and realized how much we missed the big city life. I then fulfilled the original reason for going into advertising and that was to work for a firm that called on buyers at advertising agencies selling them time on TV stations in many markets.

My career started at Katz in 1967 when people were more than a commodity. Companies were interested in more than the bottom line. They were interested in the well being of their employees and their families.

Katz was one of the largest representatives in the business and they sold TV and radio time as well as newspaper space to advertising agencies whose clients were interested in placing advertising in various markets. Katz had been started in 1888 as a newspaper rep firm and expanded with the times.

During the many crisis we had with our boys there were too many times to count that I had to be away from the office, well beyond the allowable days off and it was never an issue with management. I do not believe that would be acceptable in today's market place.

An opening became available to expand the Atlanta office in 1976 and I was promoted to Sales Manager and eventually Vice President of the continental division.

In 1986 Katz moved the Jacksonville office to Tampa and I was asked to move there and manage it. I remained there until I retired in 1995.

The business of selling TV time was cutthroat at times and could be very confrontational. Two stories come to mind that reflect how nasty it could be.

After a very difficult negotiation with one of the buyers I called on and the sales manager from the station, we left the buyers office and the station man realized that he forgot his briefcase. Rather than go back to the buyers office he said that he was going to leave it there. I had to go back and retrieve it for him.

Another station man from another market retired and when his replacement came to make sales calls I asked him what his predecessor was doing. He told me his predecessor was now taking mug shots of the criminals at the local jail when they were being booked and that he felt that he was meeting a much better class of people.

There were some exceptions to the rule on the buying side. I made lifelong friends with a real great guy named John Long. John recently passed away and will always be remembered for his faith in God and his sense of humor. His wife Diane is also one of Gods special people and I have continued to stay in touch with her since John died.

Chapter Twelve

The Adoption

When Lynda and I got engaged, we discussed how she felt about adoption if all else failed. She said she could never adopt. As they say, "never say never."

I mention this because I want anyone who feels as Lynda did to reconsider. The minute we met Ty at the adoption agency, he was our son, and he belonged to us and we belonged to him. Sometimes people would say, "Isn't he adopted?" and we had to think about it. He was always our son from day one, and we couldn't have loved him any more if he had been our biological child.

We adopted Ty in October of 1971 when he was ten months old. We had been trying to get pregnant for five years and had many miscarriages.

We were finally told by the doctors that the probability of Lynda completing a nine-month pregnancy was very slim and that we should consider adoption.

Ty was a beautiful, blue-eyed, blond-haired child. Truly, people stopped to stare at him on the street. He had Addison's disease, which is a malfunctioning adrenal gland that could easily be controlled with medication. Some people were hesitant to take a child with any medical condition, regardless of how minor it seemed. That is why we believe he had not been adopted. Adoption was easier in 1971. We discussed this medical problem with our pediatrician, and she said it was minor, but there were no guarantees in life. If she were in our position, she would adopt him. Obviously, we took her advice. It was the best decision we ever made.

The adoption agency we went through in New York City required all couples to attend a meeting in groups of about ten who had completed the adoption process.

Of the ten couples at our meeting, six of us had gotten pregnant since adopting. We were told that this was not uncommon. I am happy to say we were one of the six.

Lynda was pregnant with our daughter, Kate, who would be born in August of 1972.

Chapter Thirteen

Kate

Kate was born at the end of Lynda's second trimester and weighed two pounds. She only lived a week.

We believed her short life was due to her prematurity and the fact that the community hospital she was in was not able to handle such a small baby.

Lynda always regretted never being able to hold Kate. This would never happen today because parents are encouraged to hold their babies even if it is only once, and even if it would be postmortem.

Chapter Fourteen

Andy

Lynda got pregnant three months after Kate died, and delivered our son, Andy, also at the end of her second trimester. This time, we were prepared and had found a doctor affiliated with one of the best hospitals in New York City, Mt. Sinai Hospital.

After Kate died, my cousin John Coughlin and his wife Marion had their first child, and we went to the hospital to see mother and child.

It was very difficult for Lynda to see all the newborns in the nursery, but it gave her a firm resolve to continue to try for a viable baby.

Andy was born May 6, 1973, and he couldn't quite make Kate's weight class. He was only one and one-half pounds. His advantage was that he was at a major hospital in the city.

If you do the math, you will see that Lynda delivered babies nine months apart. It is not as barbaric as it sounds when you realize Andy was born in her sixth month, and if she had gone full-term, there would have been a year between births.

At Mt. Sinai, we met one of the best neonatologists in the country, who was a very caring and realistic man.

The first time we asked Dr. Fox if Andy would live, he said, "Let's put it this way. If he were a chicken, I wouldn't buy him yet." For almost four months, his response was "not yet." We decided this would be our code rather than having to ask "is he going to live?"

You can imagine our excitement when he finally said yes, he would buy him. This meant Andy was about to come home.

Andy developed hydrocephalus, which is fluid in the brain, because his ventricles were not circulating his spinal fluid the way they should. The only way to correct this and give Andy a shot at some kind of quality of life was brain surgery.

All the pediatric neurosurgeons at Mt. Sinai refused to perform the surgery on Andy because they felt he was too fragile and would not make it off the operating table.

Andy was now up to about four pounds, but his weight gain had mostly been in his head. If we left him this way, he would be severely brain damaged and most likely be nonfunctioning—if he survived at all.

Chapter Fifteen

Brain Surgery

After informing us that no doctor would attempt the surgery at Mt. Sinai, Dr. Fox told us he knew of a pediatric neurosurgeon at Einstein Hospital in the Bronx.

Not only was Kenneth Shulman one of the best in the country, but he had just invented a shunt that could save Andy's life and give him a shot at quality.

We requested that Dr. Fox contact Dr. Shulman and ask if he would come to Mt. Sinai and see if Andy was a candidate for his new shunt.

We found out later that in order to encourage Dr. Shulman to perform the surgery, Dr. Fox pumped Andy's incubator with excessive oxygen to make him look pinker and more able to handle the surgery. Dr. Fox knew that we wanted Andy to have a decent life and were willing to take the chance of losing him during the operation.

After examining Andy, Dr. Shulman met with us and informed us that he would perform the surgery at Einstein Hospital in the next couple of days.

Lynda and I were so excited that we jumped out of our chairs, hugged Dr. Fox and Dr. Shulman, and ran out of the room like thieves in the night. We were afraid he might change his mind.

The problem with this was that Dr. Fox had told Dr. Shulman that over the past seven weeks, he had found us to be knowledgeable and inquisitive and that he should be prepared for a barrage of intelligent questions and should anticipate spending time with us. Surprise!

Andy was transferred to Einstein Hospital in a special incubator-equipped ambulance, and the trip was the first of many hurdles we would all be faced with for many, many years.

Dr. Shulman had told us during the initial interview that the surgery was "a simple plumbing problem," but the real test would be for Andy to get the appropriate lifesaving postoperative care.

He could only promise that we would have a child to work with and that only time would tell how much brain damage Andy had sustained.

The surgery was a success, but there was so much fluid in the brain that when they put the shunt in and diverted the fluid to his abdomen, it created pressure on his diaphragm and restricted his breathing.

The only way they could assist him with breathing was to put him on a ventilator. This did the job but created a lifelong problem.

He was only about four pounds at this time, so all his organs were very small. There was not a ventilator that was the appropriate size, so they had to force a larger size than they wanted. This enabled him to breathe but created scar tissue in his airway. When they took him off the ventilator, he could not breathe, so they had to perform a tracheotomy below the scar tissue that enabled him to breathe on his own. We were told at the time that they hoped it would be temporary, but it wasn't.

Andy has had many surgeries in hopes that the trache tube could come out, but in the long run, they were only temporary solutions.

Andy has had the trache out twice—once in Atlanta for two years and once in Florida for ten years. It is now permanent unless someone comes up with a procedure that could transplant airways.

At this point, Andy appeared to be doing as well as could be expected, so Lynda and I decided to accept an invitation to fly from New York City to Miami for a long weekend as guests of Anita and Charlie MacMichal. We thought this would be a good time to regain strength and get prepared for what lies ahead.

Little did we know our troubles were just beginning, and this was only the tip of the iceberg.

Chapter Sixteen

Emergency Flight Home

We asked my sister Maryalice if she
would be willing to take care of Ty
for three days while we recuperated
in Miami. She had five children of her own,
and they were all excited about spending time with their cousin. We lived
about an hour apart, so we only saw each other during the holidays.

We flew to Miami on Friday, and on Saturday morning when we
woke, Lynda told me she had a bad feeling about Ty and would I call
Maryalice and see if he was all right.

When Maryalice answered the phone, she informed me that they
were headed out the door to take Ty to Southampton Hospital because
he was lethargic and nonresponsive. Southampton turned them away
because they had no idea as to what to do for him.

My next conversation with Maryalice was that they were taking Ty to
the hospital where his pediatrician practiced in Long Island and that we
should come home immediately. She did not tell us that he was now in a
full coma.

Charlie and Anita lived about thirty minutes from the airport, and I hesitate to estimate the number of traffic tickets Charlie would have gotten if there had been a police car on the route we took.

When we arrived, we had fifteen minutes to make our flight.

We got to the check-in, and there were a number of people ahead of us who were catching later flights, and if we waited our turn, we would never make our flight.

Charlie went to the counter and explained our situation to the clerk and asked if she would push us to the front of the line. Much to our surprise, she said no and that we must wait our turn.

Charlie is about six feet four inches tall and has a full head of prematurely pure-white hair.

After the clerk said no, Charlie stepped on the scale at the counter and asked the many people in front of us if we could go ahead because of a medical emergency. He looked almost godlike with his height and hair color, standing on the scale with his arms fully extended.

We were almost lifted over the heads of the people in front of us, and we made our flight—thanks to Charlie and a great group of strangers.

Chapter Seventeen

Reye's Syndrome

When we got in the car at the airport in New York, Maryalice and her husband, Joe, were very reserved and quiet. They finally informed us that Ty was in a coma and had been since they left the house in Montauk, Long Island.

He was to stay in that coma for six weeks, except for one time when he stopped breathing, and they had to resuscitate him. We sometimes wonder if we should have let him go, and maybe it was God's will to take him then because he knew what lay ahead.

We prayed very hard that God spare Ty no matter what the residual damage would be. As they say, "Be careful what you pray for."

Ty was diagnosed with Reye's syndrome, which is a very rare childhood disease, and if the child didn't die (which was the norm), survivors had a myriad of complications.

It initially was thought that giving a child an aspirin to combat a slight fever was the cause of Reye's. Maryalice had done this, but I recently found out that Reye's was absolutely not related to the aspirin protocol.

No one ever came up with a reason for Reye's, and the disease just went away all over the world. By the way, Ty was now at the same community hospital where his sister, Kate, died.

Chapter Eighteen

God's Grace

We now had a four-pound preemie fighting for his life in an incubator at Einstein Hospital in the Bronx, and a two-and-a-half-year-old in a coma in a community hospital in Long Island, forty-five minutes apart.

Although neither of the boys was aware of our presence, we made it a point to visit each of them every day. We didn't care what their conditions were. We never knew if just hearing our voices helped. We like to believe it did, and it made us feel better to see them.

One day when we were in the car traveling from one hospital to the other, Lynda said to me that she felt because we are all human beings, we are subject to human frailties, and that God does not inflict these crises on us but makes sure he gives us all the grace to get through them.

When we told Dr. Shulman about Ty, he said that we should transfer him to Einstein Hospital immediately because he felt they were better equipped to care for him.

We will never forget the sight of Dr. Shulman walking down the corridor of the hospital in his bloodstained scrubs with our very limp two-and-a-half-year-old in a coma in his arms saying, "Don't worry, I have him now."

I was told by my wife that Dr. Shulman was a major heartthrob among the women whose children he was caring for at the hospital, and they all thought he was gorgeous.

Every time the mothers found out he was to do rounds, all of them scampered back to their child's room where they were sleeping at night and quickly changed into fancy peignoir sets and put on their best faces. It was really quite amusing.

The pressure of the doctoring field that Dr. Shulman chose was tremendous and eventually got the best of him. He died shortly after treating our boys. What a great loss to all the children who could have used his help.

Thank you, Dr. Shulman, for what you did for our boys. I just know you were among the first to greet Ty in heaven.

Lynda and I decided that nothing would be worse than what we were going through at Einstein, and we would always try to keep a positive attitude. Despite all our problems, I believe we were able to accomplish this goal.

We now had our boys, two beds apart, in the same intensive care unit at death's door for weeks to come.

I remember once when an intern asked if she could speak to Lynda alone. The intern informed Lynda that they were all worried about her because there was no crying or yelling and screaming on the floor at the hospital during the day, and they wondered if, possibly, she didn't understand the severity of the situation. Lynda told her that there were too many life-and-death decisions that had to be made daily and that all the histrionics were reserved for the privacy of our own home.

One morning, I called the ICU at Einstein Hospital to find out what kind of a night Andy had. The nurse informed me that he was fine until three o'clock this morning. My heart stopped when she didn't continue. With great trepidation, I asked her what happened at 3:00 a.m. "Oh," she said, "I went off duty, and he was just fine."

We knew then it was time to try to get Andy back to the neonatal unit at Mt. Sinai so he could get the appropriate care. Dr. Fox took Andy under his wing again at Mt. Sinai, and things seemed to stabilize for a while.

Chapter Nineteen

 ## The Homecoming

I t was now time to get our boys home. Ty came home in early September while Andy stayed in the hospital until late October.

As it turned out, it was good that Ty came home first because we were able to concentrate on his needs and establish some routine with his care.

We thought the hard part was behind us, but it was just the beginning. Taking care of one handicapped child is a lot of work and stress, but caring for two handicapped children is impossible unless God places the right people in your path to help.

Because of the medical knowledge needed to care for either of our boys, it was necessary to hire an LPN whenever one of the boys had an appointment outside our home, and this was often. A regular babysitter or family member could not do the job.

This was in the '70s when companies considered more than the bottom line, and this included insurance companies. The company Katz used for our health insurance was not the enemy, as they are today, but did everything possible to make our lives easier.

I had often heard the saying "it took a village to raise a family." I was about to find out how true this was and how we could not have done it ourselves.

A short time after Ty came home, he was sitting with Lynda when he lifted his paralyzed left arm, let it drop to his side, and said to Lynda, "All gone."

This was from a not yet-three-year-old who had just suffered severe brain trauma, and he was letting his mom know that he was aware of what he had lost.

Chapter Twenty

Peggy

It was time to bring our entire family under one roof. Andy was now six months old and had lived in hospitals his entire life.

The day before we were to bring Andy home with a tracheotomy, we were all very excited and could not wait.

In order to complete the last piece of the puzzle, Lynda had to spend the night with him to simulate home but with backup help if needed.

The next morning when Lynda arrived home, I was waiting at the door to greet her and share the plan for Andy's arrival, and I expected her to be very excited. I could not have been more wrong.

When Lynda got out of the car, she was in tears and looked like she hadn't slept a wink. She hadn't.

She felt there was no way she could meet the needs of both of the boys because she had been up all night suctioning Andy, and he wasn't sick. This was going to be a normal routine. How was she going to be up with Andy all night and care for both of them during the day?

For the first two years, Andy slept in our bedroom so we could take turns suctioning him. There were nights when this happened every fifteen minutes. Because of the trache, Andy could not clear his throat by himself like we can, so we had to suction his airway.

Enter Peggy.

When Lynda had to take one of the boys to an appointment away from home, it was necessary that the insurance company pay for a professional nurse to take care of the other boy.

When you hired a nurse, they required a minimum of four hours, even if you needed them for only one hour.

Peggy Alves was God's first gift brought to our home. Peggy saw how impossible it was for Lynda to do what she had to twenty-four hours a day, so she agreed to stay only the amount of time needed while Lynda was out of the house. Peggy would bank the other hours for times when she was really needed, even if it was just for us to go to a movie, go out for a quick dinner, or to take a long nap.

Peggy was a young single mother with a daughter and always brought her to our house with her. They quickly became family and even went on vacations with us.

Another person that went above and beyond the call of duty was Warren Woodworth. He was Andy's ENT specialist and lived in the neighborhood.

Many times, Andy would get into a coughing fit that could only be stopped with a shot of Zylocaine directly into the trache.

It was not uncommon for this to happen in the middle of the night, and Warren always came when called, no matter what the hour.

The first Christmas the boys were home, our living room looked like a department store. Gifts for the boys came from all over the country, some from people we didn't know.

Chapter Twenty-One

Atlanta

I n 1976 when we moved to Atlanta, Lynda had to start all over again establishing a new network of doctors and caregivers. Andy was now three, and Ty was almost six.

Peggy came to the rescue once more. She volunteered to come to Atlanta for the first two weeks, thus allowing Lynda to meet with anyone, anywhere, anytime.

Two of the first people we met when we moved to our new home were a pair of twelve-year-old girls named Anna Galifianakis and Lynda Foernsler who lived in the neighborhood and were very interested in learning how to care for Ty and Andy. This amazed us because we couldn't get an adult family member or friend to take on this responsibility.

Anna went on to pursue a successful career in nursing and recently told me that caring for the boys stimulated her interest in nursing.

The girls were quick studies, and Lynda hired them to be with the boys after school so she could work around the house. Eventually, she became comfortable enough to leave the boys with them so she could do chores away from the house that didn't require a lot of time.

We had never been told that Andy had cerebral palsy until we got to Atlanta. It was a tremendous shock to us. The neurologist in Atlanta could not believe we had never been informed. This didn't change Andy's care on our part but it did present more things to us in caring for him.

Andy became the poster child for cerebral palsy in Atlanta in 1978. He had his fifteen minutes of fame riding in the back of a convertible in a holiday parade with the football coach of Georgia, Vince Dooley.

Because of Ty's paralysis, he was able to attend a special CP camp in Alabama when he was eight. We all drove Ty there and were very pleased with what was available.

As we gathered to say good-bye to Ty, one of the counselors asked us where we were going with Andy. We said he was only five, and, with his trache, we felt he was not a candidate to stay. Deep down, we felt no one was capable of taking care of him but us.

They would not let us go and told us to leave Andy and return the next day with clothes and anything else we thought he might need.

With great concern, we left our two handicapped boys with total strangers and brought Andy's clothes the next day. In six years, we had never let the boys out of our sight, much less for two weeks. They attended camp for three consecutive years.

The first year, Lynda never left the house for that two-week period because she was afraid she would miss an emergency phone call. They hadn't invented cell phones yet.

The second year, we went to a movie or dinner—never both because we didn't want to miss a call.

The third year, we went to Nassau for the two weeks, where there were no phones.

Chapter Twenty-Two

Stewart Home School

It was becoming increasingly obvious that it was impossible to be good caregivers to both boys. We felt that maybe Ty would be better served in a private facility.

We did a tremendous amount of research over a year and visited many facilities, not only in Georgia but the entire Southeast.

We saw an ad in a magazine called the *Exceptional Parent* for the Stewart Home School in Frankfurt, Kentucky, and they seemed to have everything Ty needed.

The Stewart Home School was on five hundred acres of land and, in the 1800s, had been a military school.

It was now being run by the third generation of Stewarts, so they really had their act together. They cared for two hundred children and adults who were full-time residents and attended school on campus.

Don't misunderstand; this was a very difficult decision for Lynda and me to make, and there were members of both families who thought we were doing the wrong thing and didn't hesitate to express their feelings.

Lynda and I spent many hours crying before and after Ty went to Stewart and prayed to God that we were making the right decision.

My mother and her husband, Tony, came to visit us in Atlanta just before we announced to the family that Ty would be going to the Stewart School. We told Mother and Tony at dinner the first night of this one-week stay.

Mother got up from the table, left her dinner, went to her room, and didn't come out again that night. When we woke up the next morning, Mother and Tony were sitting on their suitcases at the top of the driveway, waiting for a cab to take them to the airport. Lynda and I decided it would be fruitless to try to talk to them, so we just let them leave.

When my mother got home, she called my sister Sheila, who was living in Morocco. She asked Sheila to rescue Ty and volunteer to take him in to her family.

Sheila had done that with other children in the family, but these were children in some kind of temporary crisis.

Not only did Sheila not interfere, but she called us to tell us that she heard about our decision to send Ty to school, and she stood behind us 100 percent. She told us it was a very brave decision, and not only was Ty going to benefit, but the whole family would eventually realize it was the right and only decision to make.

There were many times as Ty's leaving got closer that I had to pull over to the side of the road because I was crying and couldn't see well.

The three of us drove Ty to school and stayed at a hotel in Lexington, Kentucky, one night before separating.

We were sitting in the lounge of the hotel enjoying family time, and the guitarist played "Lonesome Road." Much to our surprise, Andy knew all the lyrics and started to sing. When the guitarist noticed, she came over and gave him a microphone. He sang a solo! It was beautiful, and he was given a standing ovation with many a tear in the room. Remember, Andy had a trache and had to put his finger over it to sing. And he was a very slight seven-year-old.

After leaving Ty at Stewart, Lynda, Andy, and I broke down on the front porch of the school and cried in one another's arms.

Thank God we were directed to the Stewart school.

Chapter Twenty-Three

 ## Separation Anxiety

W e were not allowed to call Ty for the first three weeks and not allowed to visit him for three months after he went to the Stewart Home School. This was tough for all of us but proved to be the best plan that had withstood the test of time for three generations of Stewarts.

Despite Ty's paralysis on the left side of his body, Stewart taught Ty to swim, play basketball, and dress himself. They instilled in him a confidence we would never have been able to do and taught him to be semi-independent.

Before Ty went to Stewart, we used to watch a lot of tennis as a family. You never knew how much of what was going on around Ty that he absorbed because he was speech-impaired and could not communicate well.

During one of his visits home from school, we were hitting tennis balls over the net from the service box, and Ty hit a shot into the net. He looked at me with a silly look on his face, threw his racquet on the ground and said, "Me McEnroe" and proceeded to roll on the ground laughing.

Ty stayed at Stewart for ten years and would come home three or four times a year. After two or three days of a two-week stay at home, we would find Ty packing his bag with little treasures from home, telling us he was ready to go back to school on "me plane."

The best trips home were for Christmas because he was a Christmas Eve baby.

Chapter Twenty-Four

 ## Helen and Tony

My father passed away in 1972 of a heart attack. He was found in his car in a parking lot and never regained consciousness.

Tony Braun had been a friend of the family for forty years and had never married. He was a great guy, and the entire family was crazy about him. We always believed that Tony was in love with my mother's sister, Rita, and if Dan should predecease Rita, Tony and Rita would get married.

As it turned out, Rita died first, so it was Plan B, Helen. Please don't misunderstand; we believe Tony loved my aunt Rita and my mother equally as much. We believe he always loved the Schoen sisters, and that might have been one of the reasons he never married.

Tony lived with his mother when my father passed away and started courting my mother very soon after my father's death. My mother was sixty-three and Tony was sixty-one.

My mother said that if anyone told her she would be kissing her boyfriend good night and sending him home to his mother when she was sixty-three, she would have told them that they were crazy!

Mother told us that Tony was a very affectionate man, and she asked him one day if he was that way with his mother. He wasn't, but told her he would start to correct that immediately. The next night when he said good-bye to visit Mother, he leaned down and kissed his mother. She looked up at him in a very confused state and said, "You are never coming back." His mother was ninety-three and couldn't handle the change.

Mother and Tony were married in 1973. Mother was sixty-five and Tony was sixty-three. We kidded her about being a "cougar."

They lived in a lovely and large two-bedroom, two-bath, rent-controlled apartment in White Plains, New York. The building had converted to condos, but anyone who lived there before the conversion was allowed to stay there as renters with a controlled, small increase in rent every year.

They lived there for about twenty-five years, and every year they were there, the association lost money on their unit.

When the time came for them to move to where they could get support from family members, I called the association and made them a proposal. I thought I could convince them to move if the association offered Helen and Tony ten thousand dollars. They didn't know that Mother and Tony were going to move whether they received the so-called "buyout" or not. The association countered with an offer of six thousand dollars, and off they went.

Mother and Tony had a wonderful life together. Tony died at ninety-three, and Mother died at ninety-nine, three months short of one hundred years old.

While I am reminiscing about my mother, I am reminded of the time she felt that she was saved by an angel.

At age eighty-five, she unsteadily climbed a three-step step stool in her kitchen to put away some dishes in an overhead cabinet. The step stool was located in front of an open window three stories above the ground. She felt herself lose her balance and knew that she was headed out the window to the street.

The next thing she knew, she was standing in her dining room about ten feet from the open window. She felt in a very euphoric state and had no bruises or bumps and felt better than she had in a very long time. She always believed that her angel caught her and gently placed her in the living room unharmed.

The only damage was the broken dishes on the kitchen floor.

Chapter Twenty-Five

 ## Andy's Many Surgeries

Up to age eleven, Andy had multiple surgeries with an end goal of removing the trache permanently. In 1984 in Atlanta, it was removed.

In 1986 I was asked to open the Tampa office for my company, and we made another move.

Just before the move, it became evident that Andy was having trouble breathing, and he went for another procedure to help him breathe easier. When he went under anesthesia, none of us knew that they were going to have to retrache him. This all happened the day the movers came to move us to Clearwater, Florida.

To say that Andy was upset when he came out of the anesthesia is an understatement. He was moving to a new neighborhood, a new school, and would meet new children, many of whom, if any at all, had ever seen an indwelling tracheotomy. Andy's dream in life was to be Joe Banana, one of a bunch, but this was never going to be.

We have always been proud of Andy for his ability to adjust but never more proud than at that time.

The hospital Andy often went to was Egleston Children's Hospital in Atlanta where our neighbor and very good friend, Willis Williams, was chief of surgery. Whenever Andy went in for a procedure, Willis made sure Andy had the best of care.

I called ICU to ask how Andy was doing one day and if I could talk to him. I heard the head nurse call out, "Has anyone seen Andy?" Andy had gone for a ride on a bike that he had commandeered from the playroom. I think he thought he was Eloise at the Plaza. Remember, he was in ICU.

Chapter Twenty-Six

 ## Andy's Comfort Zone

As I mentioned earlier, Andy spent the first six months of his life in the hospital, and stays at various hospitals where we lived were commonplace. Some of the stays were lengthy.

The number of days Andy has spent in the hospital is astronomical and almost impossible to calculate. These stays were due to shunt revisions, shunt infections, eight back surgeries, innumerable tracheal surgeries, heel cord extensions, pneumonia, and abdominal surgery. He became a frequent flier at many hospitals in various cities.

Most stays were at least two weeks, and one I remember was about six weeks when they had to take the shunt out because the bacteria had colonized in the plastic. They had to put a bolt in his head and drain the fluid thru a tube outside his body and surgically implant the other end of the tube in his abdomen until the infection cleared up. I remember, at the end of this particular stay, Andy refused to go home. I could understand why he felt this way.

He had young, pretty nurses with him 24-7, and they were not a great deal older than he was. He had three meals a day, his own TV, and all the attention he wanted. Many nurses would spend some of their lunch break visiting with him, especially the night staff. As a patient at All Children's Hospital, Andy was well beyond the acceptable age limit.

Andy and Ty both had their haircuts by a wonderful stylist named Rosie. She always made a big production when the boys entered the salon.

When Andy's stays at All Children's Hospital went beyond his time for a haircut, Rosie would collect her tools, hop on the back of her boyfriend's motorcycle, and give him free haircuts in his room in the hospital. Rosie was another gift in our lives.

Andy has no fear of hospitals and has wonderful memories of his stays there despite the discomfort.

Chapter Twenty-Seven

New Beginning

When we moved to Clearwater, Florida, in 1986, Lynda had to reestablish a complicated new network of doctors and caregivers.

One of the surgeons we heard about was Peter Orobello, who had just moved to All Children's Hospital in St. Petersburg from the University Hospitals of Cincinnati. His specialty was tracheal reconstruction. Obviously, this was Lynda's first call.

The many surgeries were eventually successful, and Andy's trache was once again removed in 1998. These surgeries occurred over an eight-year time frame. The following letter written by Andy to his surgeons at All Children's Hospital gives insight as to how he has felt almost his entire life.

7-29-93

Dear Drs. Orobello and Andrews,

I really appreciate the job that you guys are doing to try and ewe me a chance at a better life than it has been for the past 18-20 years. To tell you the truth my life has been a living hell because I got picked on and laughed at alot through the years and it really hurt me inside to always feel that no one accepted me-for who I was when I was a little kid. Even in middle school people used to make fun of me because I have C.P. and a trach so no one thought that I would amount to anything. I was once told by a P.E. coach that I could not be on the track team because of my C.P. and because he thought I was too slow and also because of my trach. That really upset me alot. I've had a lot of emotional difficulties through the years because I was picked on and it really made me feel like I could never play anything and be good at it. To this day, some people can not accept me but others admire me for all the stuff I have been through just as both of you have done, it really makes me feel good inside to know that I have 2 caring doctors at my side. I want Dr. Andrews there when you pull out my trach because you both made it possible. Once again thanks for a second chance at a new life I have wanted for the past 7 years. your

Sincerely

Andrew F. Barrett

59

After Andy's trache was removed, he was able to attend a fabulous summer camp for eight consecutive summers. The camp was Camp Rockmont outside of Asheville, North Carolina, in Black Mountain. Andy was the first handicapped camper they took, and it helped Andy with self-image a great deal. He even went back one year to work in the kitchen but had a congenital back defect that made it impossible to stand for any length of time.

Andy even got to attend the Stewart Home School for a year, but finances forced us to bring him home. This was the eleventh year we were paying college-like tuition for the boys.

After ten years without his trache, for the second time, Andy's airway started to close up again and he had to be retrached. It appears, barring a miracle or some new dramatic surgical procedure, it is in to stay.

Again we are very proud of the way Andy has handled all his setbacks, and when his time comes, he will be on Ty's express train to heaven.

Chapter Twenty-Eight

Andy's Apartment

Andy was having a difficult time living on his own. Regardless of how much he wanted to, it just wasn't working. I am sorry to say that there is always someone around the corner ready to take advantage of lonely people.

We tried to teach him basic living skills, but when you have two handicapped children in the same house, it is sometimes more efficient to do things yourself rather than stop and teach.

We decided that since the Stewart Home School had done such wonderful things for Ty, that maybe they could help Andy.

Before he could reap the full benefits that Stewart offered, we had to withdraw him after only one year.

When he returned home, Lynda immediately applied for HUD housing for him because he was unable to work and was trying to live on government assistance. This wasn't working. The problem was that there was a two- to three-year waiting list for affordable housing at the time.

Just about a little over two years after Lynda applied for Andy, she was hired by a company that shared office space with the agency that controlled the housing Andy had applied for.

On Lynda's lunch breaks in a shared cafeteria, she became friendly with the person who controlled the housing assignments.

One day, in passing, Lynda told her that Andy had applied for housing over two years ago and would she please find out where he stood on the waiting list.

The woman called Lynda later in the day and asked if she could stop by her office. Apparently, Andy was never put on the waiting list, but they had all the paperwork that had been done, and according to the date of the paperwork, he was next on the list for housing—and they had one that was perfect for him. They said he could have it as soon as they did the necessary work to spruce it up.

Andy moved into the apartment and has lived there for ten years.

Lynda had heart surgery in 2005 and lost her job due to the length of time it took for her to recover because of some very serious complications.

Andy mentioned this to the woman who assigned the housing, and they had an opening for someone on a part-time basis, which could eventually become full time. This was just what Lynda was looking for, so she went to work for them.

The angel hit a home run—housing for Andy and, a short time later, employment for Lynda.

Chapter Twenty-Nine

 ## Sandy

Sandy has been Andy's caregiver for almost ten years and is another human doing angels' work.

Sandy is paid by the government to help Andy for a total of no more than thirty hours a week. This help is meant to be in assisting him shopping, with doctor appointments, and teaching him daily living skills.

I know for a fact that Sandy is with Andy for a minimum of one hundred and fifty hours a month, which means that she is not paid for about thirty hours a month.

She cleans his apartment every day, takes his laundry to her home and washes and dries it, takes him out to eat regularly (sometimes at her own expense), prepares meals for him over the weekend that he can eat during the week, and gets him out of his apartment often just to give him a change of scenery.

Sandy came to Florida almost twenty years ago when her son hurt her beyond repair. He was to marry into a high-society family and told Sandy that he was uncomfortable inviting her to the wedding, and he hoped that she understood. She packed her bags, left town, and never looked back.

One time, in her old hometown, she read about a man whose car had been stolen and had to quit his job. Because he had a handicap, he was unable to take public transportation. Sandy gave this stranger her three-thousand-dollar car and started to take public transportation herself.

Recently, Sandy was given a twenty-dollar gift certificate to a fast-food restaurant. This was a gift from one of the people she helps for free on a regular basis.

She was in that restaurant with Andy one day and was watching four young boys take turns refilling a soda cup and returning to the table for all to share. Sandy went over to their table and gave them her gift certificate. The playwrite Clare Booth Luce said that no good deed goes unpunished. When Sandy was leaving the store, she overheard one of the young boys talking on the phone. He said that this old lady had given them a gift card. Sandy is only sixty years old and looks even younger.

An elderly lady recently moved in next door to me, and when I carried her groceries in to her apartment, I saw how much she was unable to care for herself. I told my new neighbor that I had a friend who could clean her apartment for her at a very reasonable rate, and if she wanted, I would have Sandy come by and give her an estimate as to what she would charge her.

When Sandy went, it was worse than what I had seen on the surface. She was storing garbage in the refrigerator because she couldn't walk the thirty yards to the trash room. She also had not done laundry for the two months she had lived there, nor had she changed her linens during that time.

Sandy is now cleaning for her once a week, taking her laundry and doing it at her own home, and she has refused to accept any money from the lady for everything she does. Remember, this is a total stranger to Sandy, who Sandy felt needed help. I know that there is family somewhere who just dropped her off to care for herself.

Another great person doing angel work.

Chapter Thirty

Angels in Our Lives

We have always believed that God watches over us all the time. Two incidents occurred in Atlanta that reinforced this belief.

Lynda and I were having dinner at a Chinese restaurant after a particularly stressful day over a surgical decision we had made for Andy. Lynda opened her fortune cookie, and it said, "Job well done." It turned out it was a good decision.

The second time we heard from our guardian angel was on a trip to Amelia Island, Florida, where we had a condo on the beach and often drove there, sometimes just for the weekend.

This particular trip, Andy and I were to drive down and Lynda was to fly later in the week. Ty was at Stewart. Andy had been vomiting for a few days, and his pediatrician assured us it was not a shunt problem but a virus. A blocked shunt can create tremendous headaches and vomiting because the spinal fluid is not draining to the abdomen properly and causes pressure in the brain.

Andy and I made it to Valdosta, Georgia, which was about halfway. We usually drove all the way in one day, about eight hours, but Andy still wasn't feeling well. I decided to see how he was going to be in the morning and plan whether to return home by car, proceed as planned, or fly Andy home and have Lynda meet him at the airport. The nausea continued during the night, so I decided to have him fly home on the next flight.

While showering in the morning, I started to drop the shampoo bottle and grabbed it with both hands and squeezed. I looked down on the shower floor, and for an instant, the shampoo formed a smiley face that quickly washed away. I felt this was a sign that I had done the right thing in having Andy fly home by himself.

When Lynda picked him up at the Atlanta airport, she took him directly to Egleston Hospital where the surgeon performed emergency surgery to relieve the pressure on the brain because his shunt was indeed blocked, and this could have caused more problems unless corrected immediately.

You will never convince me that both of these events were not direct communication from God. We are all presented with these, and we just have to pay attention.

After Ty passed away, there were three incidences that can only be explained by direct communication from the afterlife.

As I said earlier, Ty lived in a group home and attended a day program. They sent a lunch box with all the residents every day and kept them all in a box in the kitchen. The night Ty passed away, they removed his lunch box from the container where all the lunch boxes for the residents were kept and put it on the counter. The staff at the group home assured that no one had been in the kitchen during the night, but when they went to prepare breakfast for everyone, Ty's lunch box had been put back among the others.

Ty never went through puberty, so even at thirty-eight years old when he died, he looked like an early teen. The man that took over Ty's room came out to the staff one night and told them that a young boy would not let him open his window. He had never met Ty, so the man did not know what he looked like, and Ty knew it was against the rules of the house to open windows.

Lynda and I distributed Ty's cremains in front of the beach house in Hampton Bays, Long Island, where he spent his summers. It was the

Saturday before the annual Christmas party at his group home, which we were to attend despite how painful it might be for all of us when we got home.

At the party, I asked if Ty had made his presence known anytime recently and was told that on the previous Saturday at twelve noon, the lights flickered in his room only and not the rest of the house. This was the exact time we were distributing his cremains at the beach.

Chapter Thirty-One

 # Lynda's Angel

One experience with an actual angel happened in Clearwater, Florida. We lived on the eighth floor of a condo, and Lynda had stopped to do some shopping after a very trying day at All Children's Hospital where Andy had surgery on his shunt, which made him disoriented, and we were worried that this might be permanent. It wasn't.

When the elevator door at the condo opened on the first floor, a strange man was on it and made no attempt to get off. Having lived in New York for so many years, Lynda had become very aware of things that could present a dangerous situation. The man offered to help her with her groceries, and her gut feeling was to get on with him. As the door of the elevator closed, the man said that he could see she had a bad day but not to worry, everything was going to be all right. And would she like to pray with him? She said it was the most beautiful prayer that she ever heard. When the elevator doors opened on the eighth floor, Lynda bent down to pick up her groceries, and the man had disappeared and could not be seen anywhere on the floor. She became aware of the most beautiful aroma of flowers that she had ever experienced. Lynda told this story to a priest friend of ours, Father Eric Peters, and he told her that angels have a smell more beautiful than anything we experience on earth.

Chapter Thirty-Two

Road Trip

Returning to golf is one of the ways I am trying to cope with the dreadful loneliness in my life. My game can be good depending on which of my games shows up at the time. Also, writing this book, whether it be published or not, is great therapy.

I have been asking my patron saint, Saint Jude, for help to present opportunities to help me move on with my life. Not only has he stepped in, but I believe Lynda had a hand in what happened.

I recently made a four-week road trip to scatter Lynda's cremains in areas of the country she requested, and to visit family and friends. The trip started in Atlanta where I visited Lynda's brother, Fred Schmitt, and his wife, Marilyn. Every day consisted of a trip either to the driving range or to the PGA golf store, or a round of golf. A great beginning! Lynda loved her brother and sister-in-law very much, as do I, and would be very proud that we are maintaining our relationship.

The next stop was Hendersonville, North Carolina, where Lynda and I tried to visit at least once a year. We always picnicked at a stream in the Mount Pisgah National Forest when we went there, and this was the first place I distributed some of her cremains. My sister, Sheila, and her husband, Harvey Roth, drove over from Ocean City, Maryland, to be there for the last picnic at the stream.

We spent three days in the Asheville area while I showed them where we lived in Ashville and ate at Lynda's favorite restaurant, The Sunset Grill, at the world-famous Grove Park Inn.

We then returned to Ocean City where I distributed more cremains at the beach. A couple of years before, Lynda spent what was to be her last day at the beach and never forgot the calm waves and beautiful sand.

I then visited with friends, Len and Cindy Graziano, in Stamford, Connecticut; my sister Maryalice in Port Chester, New York; and my friends, Matt and Joan Cavanagh, in Merrick, Long Island. My nephew, Michael Messemer, flew to Florida from East Hampton, New York, for Lynda's funeral and invited me to stay with him for a few days if I did in fact take the dream trip.

This worked out great because I promised I would distribute some of the cremains on the beach in front of the old homestead. (Lynda and I distributed some of Ty's ashes at the same site five years earlier.) On to East Hampton, which was only one hour away from Hampton Bays.

Since Lynda and I moved often, I never got to spend much time with my nieces and nephews, and I was looking forward to getting to know Michael and, of course, play golf.

One night when Michael and I were having a magnificent meal he prepared and a bottle of wine, Michael told me there had been something bothering him for forty-one years, and he wanted to finally get it off his chest.

When Ty was staying with his family, the kids drew lots to see who would be the doctor and give him aspirin for the fever, and Michael was the lucky one. He was thirteen years old and always felt that he had a hand in the fact that Ty got Reye's syndrome and was so handicapped. This blew me away!

I tried to assure him that neither Lynda nor I felt anyone had any responsibility in Ty's illness. I emphasized that he only gave him an aspirin as we would have done at home. I think I was able to help him because when we parted, we hugged, and he said that this had been a life-changing experience. I hope he meant that he was relieved of the misconception of his part in Ty's illness and knew that Lynda and I both loved him very much.

After I returned home, I was given more information about Reye's and aspirin and will explain in the next chapter.

After my time with Michael, I returned to Sheila in Ocean City for five more days. I was gone exactly one month and had put 3,200 miles on the car. Everywhere I went, I was treated like a king and felt Lynda was with me the entire time.

I know this is silly, but it was important to me that I kept the box of Lynda's cremains on the passenger seat the entire trip. The ride was always the best part of our vacations.

Chapter Thirty-Three

Renewing Old Friendships

When I returned home, I started to go to the driving range on a very regular basis. One day, a man passed me in the parking lot, and we said hello. It turned out that I played tennis with him every Monday night for ten years, but since I left the club fifteen years ago, I had not seen him. Most importantly, his name was Bob Morelli, and he had been the boys' pediatrician. We went to hit balls, and I looked behind me, and there was another man I had not seen for fifteen years who had been a business associate. You will never convince me that God, Saint Jude, and Lynda did not have a hand in this chance meeting.

What are the odds that the three of us would be at the same location at the same time? Most importantly, when Bob and I said good-bye, he mentioned Ty and Reye's syndrome. I did not bring it up. He told me that he never believed the supposed connection between aspirin and Reye's. He and many of his colleagues prescribed the aspirin protocol for a child when they had a fever, and none of them ever saw a case of Reye's. Not only that, but aspirin is still being prescribed—but Reye's has completely disappeared worldwide.

I also believe Lynda brought us together because she wanted me to be able to give Michael some more proof that he is in no way responsible for Ty's condition.

Bob, George Chism, and I have all agreed to call each other for a golf date. Thanks, Lynda!

Chapter Thirty-Four

A Very Brave Decision

Some doctors depend on charts and test results as their only diagnostic tools. Others use a combination of the above in addition to intuitive feelings. Lynda was privileged to be under the care of the latter. Dr. Lang Lyn was Lynda's cardiologist in Clearwater, and if it had not been for her intuition, I would have lost Lynda in 2005. Dr. Lyn gave us eight more years together!

Although all Lynda's tests showed her heart and arteries were functioning properly, Dr. Lyn did not feel comfortable with her demeanor, so she scheduled Lynda for a catheterization. She was scheduled for Friday, May 5, 2005. While doing the cath study, Dr. Lyn discovered that three of Lynda's arteries were blocked, and she needed open-heart surgery immediately. They wouldn't even let her go home for the weekend and kept her in the hospital until Monday morning when they could schedule the surgery.

Not only did they do a triple bypass, but they removed a tumor from her heart and repaired the mitral valve.

The recovery did not go well. Lynda spent twenty-one days in intensive care during which time she experienced kidney and lung failure, which eventually caused her death. They had to put Lynda back on the ventilator after two weeks of having been off it, and she later said this was worse than any portion of the surgery or recovery.

In 2008, Lynda was diagnosed with pulmonary arterial hypertension, which is a rare and terminal illness. There were medications available to try to prolong the inevitable, but people with PAH usually survived two to three years.

The medication for PAH is quite unique. They initially prescribed Viagra and Cialis, but both of these put Lynda into cardiac arrest. The one that finally helped to some degree was Tyvaso and cost six thousand dollars a month. Once again, God was looking out for us, and we found an organization that helped in cases like this. Lynda was on Tyvaso for about two and a half years and then her body started to break down. She went into kidney failure and wound up on dialysis three times a week. After each treatment, she became weaker and wound up unable to walk the twenty feet from the car to her chair at dialysis or at home.

This—combined with being on oxygen 24-7, a CPAP machine at night, and having frequent diabetic crashes—made her life miserable, but she always had a smile on her face and a positive attitude. Strangers never knew how sick she was.

Lynda never complained and tried to do more than she was capable of doing. I believe that if Lynda had her way, she would have died in the kitchen while preparing a full Christmas feast for as many family members and friends as we could fit in the house.

A couple of weeks before Lynda went to be with our son Ty and daughter, Kate, she requested that I contact a local priest whom we didn't know but always enjoyed his homilies.

Later, Father Jack Marino told me that when asked to make these kinds of visits, he usually spent no more than fifteen minutes with the family. He spent about two hours with Lynda and really got to know her. This was beautifully reflected in his homily at her funeral service.

Although I told Lynda many times that if she decided she could no longer handle her illnesses, that whatever her decision, I would support her 100 percent.

I found out that she was seeking permission from a higher authority, and Father Jack told her that everything she was doing to stay alive was more than God expected of her. If she wished to discontinue all the extreme measures being used to keep her alive, God understood.

That night, which was a Wednesday, Lynda said she wanted to start to go through her clothes and give a lot of them away. I should have known that the end was near.

Lynda was under the care of Suncoast Hospice at this time, and on Sunday, three days after visiting with Father Jack, she was unable to get out of bed and requested that she go to the hospice care facility.

When Lynda blew me a kiss from the back of the ambulance while I was standing at our front door, I should have known this was more than just an "I love you." It was the beginning of her final journey, and she knew she would never return home.

She met with the doctor at hospice, he informed her that if she discontinued her medications and procedures, he felt she would have a week to ten days to live. Lynda told the doctor that she was comfortable with her decision, and we all prepared for the end.

Lynda always said that she had no fear of dying and going to heaven, she just didn't want to be there for the process.

Chapter Thirty-Five

 ## Lynda's Last Days

The last week Lynda was alive was almost as if she attended her own funeral service. People came from California, Connecticut, South Carolina, Maryland, Georgia, and different areas of New York. Our friend Kitty Howe, who could not make it from Michigan, was represented by her daughter who lived in St. Petersburg. Lynda was very aware they were all there.

When Lynda was about three days from the end, in a semiconscious state, she told me she wanted to go home. This surprised me because she always said that she never wanted to die at home. I mentioned this to a very good friend from hospice, Marge Morris, and she said that she believed Lynda meant home to God. That made more sense to me.

Lynda died exactly one week after deciding to "pull the plug." I was blessed to have my sisters with me at the end. Lynda's brother came from Atlanta for the funeral service because he and his wife had just visited three weeks earlier.

During their visit, Lynda heard me quietly talking to Marilyn, her sister-in-law, in the kitchen, and said, "Don't whisper!" I told Lynda that as we had often discussed, I believed she would not make it to the holidays. As it turned out, she didn't make it to the Fourth of July.

I thought watching Lynda die was the worst thing I would have to face in my life, but I was wrong.

There was a conclusion to the dying process, but there is no conclusion in sight to the terrible void and loneliness after she had gone.

The grieving may subside, but the grief never ends.

Chapter Thirty-Six

Hours To Live

It was the one call no parent ever wants to receive. Morton Plant Hospital in Clearwater Florida was calling me from Intensive Care to tell me about my son Andy. Sound familiar. It should, because this is the way I began "Everywhere An Angel" but this time they were telling me that Andy had passed the crisis and it seemed that he was going to survive. It was almost six years from the day that I got the call about Ty.

Andy has been addicted to prescription pain medications and this is not the first time he has taken too many but it is the closest he has come to not surviving.

Thursday night, he called me to inform me that his tracheotomy tube had accidentally fallen out and asked me what he should do. I told him that he had to call 911 and have them come and put it back in. Apparently they could not get it back so they took him to Morton Plant Hospital, in Clearwater. He called me again at 930am and told me that he was ready to go home and requested if I could give him a ride home. I found out later that it did not just fall out but that he took it out because he did not want it in anymore. In the 30-some years he has had it in, he never did this. I believe that it was a combination of the drugs he had taken at home that made him think unclearly and during a recent stay at the hospital a respiratory therapist told him that he should be able to get it out.

When I picked him up at the hospital, his speech was a little slurred but I thought it might be because of some medication they gave him at the E.R.

His caregiver, Sandy called me about two hours after I had dropped Andy off, to tell me that Andy was lethargic and nonresponsive and that he had taken all the meds that he was to take for the whole day all at one time. Some were sleeping pills, muscle relaxers and anxiety pills to be spread out until bedtime, not taken all at once.

Whether he took the pills all at once because they made him feel better or it was an attempted suicide we will never know. Andy swears that it was not a suicide attempt. We called the paramedics for the second time that day and they transported him to the E.R. at Morton Plant

The inability to determine whether it was a suicide attempt or an accidental overdose created a problem I was not aware of. If someone is admitted under questionable circumstances the E.R. is required to perform drastic measures to save their life despite a do not resuscitate order because if they didn't do everything under their power to save his life it could be considered enabling his suicide attempt. I think that I would consider this to be something like a suicide by cop only it could be called suicide by hospital.

Andy is still in I.C.U (3 days) because they weren't able to stabilize his blood pressure or electrolytes and he can't be sent back to the floor until this is accomplished.

Looking back on the last month or so, I realize Andy has not been clean and sober as he has professed and has fallen off the wagon a couple of times. I am sorry to say that I no longer feel that he can be trusted to live on his own. It appears that he needs to be in a setting where he can be monitored 24/7. I also believe that Andy is just starting to feel the loss of his best friend and mom, Lynda and this is contributing to his reaching out for something more to ease the pain.

Andy is a gray area person which means he is border line on being able to care for himself. He has seen the community that lives in group homes and adamantly refuses to be classified as a group home resident. He is right in some ways but wrong in so many others.

I believe that there is some sort of living arrangements available to him that will allow him to lead a normal life but with stricter supervision. His caregiver Sandy goes to his house everyday and leaves only enough medicines for that day but he is taking so many inappropriate medications that if he should take one days allocation all at once, as he did, he could overdose. In some way I blame the system because they enable him to almost get anything he wants by going to different Doctors. He knows which doctor to call for which medication and there is no source monitoring his total intake.

Andy has now been released to the floor and will be returning home in a couple of days. It is times like this I really feel the loss of Lynda. She was so good at times like this and usually knew exactly where to go for the correct help. I can only hope that some of her knowledge rubbed off on me.

Every time I think that I have completed "Angels" another crisis occurs and I have to add a paragraph or chapter. Let's hope this chapter has a happy ending.

I feel Andy did not want to kill himself but is desperately reaching out for help. I only hope that I can find it for him. Andy is desperately afraid of change, more so than the rest of us. This is part of his disability.

Epilogue

Attached is something Lynda's good friend and soul mate, Dawn Wells (who was Mary Ann on *Gilligan's Island*), wrote. Dawn was not able to be present at the service, but was able to say good-bye at the hospice care center.

I ended Lynda's eulogy with the attached entitled "Gone From My Sight" written by Henry Van Dyke, because boating and sailing were things she loved.

Lynda Barrett—who I knew for thirty-five years—was the woman I respected the most as a friend, wife, mother, and confidant.

She was smart, funny, optimistic, strong, an informed patient and perfect hostess.

She taught and lived life's lessons, took charge of her life, and defined the word *marriage*.

She was wise, truthful, filled with faith and love, and a great companion. She was kind, had taste, and knew right from wrong. She was never lazy, deceitful, or indifferent. Whether miles or time separated us, there was never a moment she wasn't in my heart.

She played the cards of life dealt her with grace, faith, strength, humor, and insight.

The love she and Tom shared was rare and blessed. Andy and Ty were raised by an angel.

She will be captain of the team of angels surely sitting at God's side. Someday I hope to meet her there. God bless you, friend.

Dawn Wells

Gone From My Sight

I am standing upon the seashore. A ship at my side spreads her white sails to the morning breeze and starts for the blue ocean. She is an object of beauty and strength. I stand and watch her until, at length, she hangs like a speck of white cloud just where the sea and sky come to mingle with each other.

Then someone at my side says: "There, she is gone!"

"Gone where?"

Gone from my sight. That is all. She is just as large in mast and hull and spar as she was when she left my side, and she is just as able to bear the load of living freight to her destined port.

Her diminished size is in me, not in her. And just at the moment when someone at my side says: "There, she is gone!" There are other eyes watching her coming, and other voices ready to take up the glad shout: "Here she comes!"

And that is dying.

Henry Van Dyke

Bon voyage, Winnie!

Acknowledgments

God
St. Jude
Lynda Barrett
Andy Barrett
Helen Messemer Thomas
Maryalice Barrett
Sheila Barrett Roth
Harvey Roth
Marge Morris
Ursula Barrett Johnson
Ellen Coughlin

Biography

Thom Barrett was born in the Bronx in 1937 when it was still fashionable. His grandfather achieved great wealth in the automobile business but lost it all by the end of World War II.

Thom was an advertising executive in New York City, Atlanta, and Tampa and retired in 1995 from the same company he worked for since 1967.

At seventy-six, he is not the oldest first-time author in the family. His paternal aunt, Ursulla Barrett Johnson, was published for the first time at the age of eighty-two. If you want to learn more about the Barretts prior to WWII read "Apples On A Lilac Tree" by Ursula Barrett Johnson.

Thom attended Mount Saint Michael High School in the Bronx and Iona College in New Rochelle, New York.